# G.P.S
# God's Promise for
# Salvation

*Biblical Doctrine and Christian Living*
*Series*

## Dedication

I dedicate this book in Loving Memory of my Grandparents, Iddo and Nellie Lane.

To my parents Pastor John and Mattie Lane, my Grandmother Mary Ward. My heart can't express words of gratitude for prayers and support for years of love and a nurturing atmosphere.

To my siblings John Eric and Sharon, thanks for just being you!

Love you!

# Acknowledgements

I express thanks to my wife, Gervia and my children Jasmine, Schelby, Phillip Jr. and Noah. Thank you for your patience as I worked on this project.

Huge thank you to Andre and Benita Smith! Words cannot express your years of friendship, laughter and tears. Thank you for your support during this project.

Thank You to Pastor Rodney Maiden for your contribution on this project. You have been a blessing for years and I learned so much from you and my family at Providence Baptist Church. Thank you and praise God for you.

Dr. A Charles Bowie, *and the East Mount Zion Baptist Church family. To Dr Roland Crowder; and The Second Calvary Baptist Church family. To my Pastor George Ellison; and The Messiah Baptist Church family. My co-laborers whom I served with in ministry, Bless you. To Pastor John H Lane Sr. and Charity Baptist Church; thank you for your support.*

# Foreword

*Every new believer needs to be instructed on how to grow in the faith. Every church needs a manual on how to instruct a new believer to become spiritually mature. Rev. Phillip Lane has put together a book that will do just that. From salvation to spiritual maturity. This manual helps the instructor to explain to every Christian the basics of salvation and what God expects from each one of us as we deepen our walk with him. Congratulations to Rev. Lane for his work of putting this manual together. A great tool for any instructor who wishes to take new believers to the next level.*

*Rodney Maiden,*

*Senior Pastor of Providence Baptist Church*

## My Prayer

My prayer for you the reader is that you find hope in your relationship with God. Whether you're a new member of a church seeking more understanding; or have questions that have not been answered. If you're an individual who has little exposure to the church experience; or want to learn of God's greatest gift of love for his creation, this book is for you.

*"Lord, I pray as the reader goes through this book you open up their understanding. I pray that they keep the truths of your word and your love for us. Let their hearts embrace and accept your message of hope for our lives,"*

*Amen*

# Table of Contents

# Part I

# Who Is God?

First by definition we can define God and believe he exists by evidence of self revelation to man. He shows himself through his creation (Genesis 1:1-2:2). One of Gods most special revelations to man is through his word, the scriptures.

The Bible provides proof of his existence; but shows the evidence of Him as eternal, Genesis 1:1 shows His presence "In the Beginning God"... The Bible is his word and his creation recognize and hear him *"They heard the voice of the Lord God walking in the garden in the cool of the day"* Genesis 3:8a.

This trumps the idea I had as a child about God being this voice in the sky with the sun as His backdrop. I know what made me think this way, over the years always hearing God answers prayer more than Biblical doctrine. So my ideology of God became skewed. Is God some genie in a bottle being there when I want or need something "Poof?" there! Oh by the way God can get "Poof?" Thanks God! Of course not! Many times I've heard people describe and advertise God as such and it is wrong. It is an embarrassment to God and who we represent.

It is important to realize that the view of God is different in a **non-Christian** perspective. Here are some of the views.

**These are Non-Christian Views:**

**Atheism:** Denies any belief in any God or gods.

**Agnosticism:** Claims that the existence of God is unknown and unknowable.

**Polytheism:** Belief in many gods.

**Pantheism:** god is everything and everything is god.

**Zoroastrian:** Believes in two opposing gods one good and one evil.

**Deism:** Belief in God, but believes he has no relationship with his creation. Call this an absentee landlord/Creator.

**Theism:** Prefer a relationship with any other god than the God (Elohim) of the Bible.

There are other views about God and as time goes on others will surface but they deny the truth of who God is and His revelation to his creation.

Since we've look at a few of the worldviews lets go into what the Bible Says. We believe in God (Elohim: Hebrew for God which shows plurality). The church believes and teaches our "Triune God" or Trinity (3 in 1). We believe in one God and he operates as one but has three distinct persons and role.

The GodHead

Father

Son                              Holy Spirit

Notice this triangle; on each corner you see the names of each member of the Godhead. It remains one triangle with three distinct corners. This never changes the oneness of its fundamental nature, but each corner has a distinct work or role making them equal in essence. I will discuss their roles further within this book.

Here are the attributes that makes our God stands out from the worldviews that exist.

## Attributes

God is self existing, which means no being can take credit for the existence of God. God tells us in the scriptures He is the "I am" Exodus 3:14; but before that was stated and time had a beginning there was Elohim/God Genesis 1:1; John 1:1. God is eternal, the everlasting God Genesis 21:33; Lord of host Isaiah 44:6. Alpha and Omega Revelations 1:8.

God is:

**Omnipotent**: This means all powerful. Nothing is impossible with God. It shows God's sovereignty to rule as he pleases. Example: God created the heavens and the earth in Genesis 1:1 but destroyed his creation by flood in Genesis 6:1-8. Only God has this absolute authority and no one can make such a claim but God.

That's what makes God Omnipotent.

God is:

**Omniscient:** This means all knowing. He understands all things, aware of all things and has absolute wisdom about all things. Who can make such a claim? I can't, nor can any created beings; regardless of what they know. Their knowledge had to be obtained from a source outside of their nature. Job questioned God and when God stepped up to question Job's understanding Job admitted, I should be silent (Ref. Job 38:1-10 full reference chapter 38-41).

God is:

**Omnipresent:** This means that God is all present (Psalms 137:7-12, Isaiah. 6:3). God is always with us. We can never escape his presence. God is not limited to space or time, because he's eternal. So it's good news when I need the Lord I create an atmosphere for our Holy God to come and help me in my time of trouble, or my time of blessing. He's where I need Him when I need Him. Thank you, for your nature of being omnipresent.

God is:

**Holy**: God is absolute purity. He is sinless and does not have the capability to sin. He wants his creation to be as he is Holy (Leviticus 19:2) The Lord God alone is Holy (Revelations. 15:3, 4). God associates with holiness. Even demons recognize the holiness of God (Mark 1:24). God takes this so serious that he gave us his Holy Spirit; after receiving Jesus by faith. The Spirit's job is to make us holy (John 14:26, I Peter 1:13-16). God inhabits holiness and wants his creation to be holy so we may have fellowship with Him.

God is:

**Righteous**: The Holiness of God requires judgment for sin and the sinner punished. Righteousness or justice demands a response from God. It's God's way of addressing sin with His creation (Romans 1:32; 2:8, 9). We must remember God is a Holy God and has the right to judge sin. He can judge sin because he declared a penalty for disobedience to his word Genesis 2:16, 17; Deuteronomy 32:4. We should not be fooled; God's justice is sure about His word.

God is:

**Love**: Our creator is a loving God. Just as one can say they've experience the love and care from a family member; God's love surpasses it. Love describe who God is (II Corinthians. 13:11). His most notable act of love is through the gift of His begotten son (John 3:16).

We can never take for granted that God loves his creation. God's loving nature provides for us salvation. His being is to show that example for us to duplicate toward each other. God is love.

## The Godhead

*"For in him dwelleth all the fullness of the Godhead bodily,"* Colossians 2:9

We believe in the eternal Godhead. We believe that He is divine. A being not like the imaginations of men; but the true and living God that no man has seen in the fullness of His glory (Acts 17:29; Colossians 1:14-17).

Since time came into existence man has never been able to place any definition on Him outside of God revealing himself (Genesis 1:1). Our great God, in three persons. Elohim is plural making this very important explaining the Triune God. Scripture even shows evidence of his plurality of personhood.

In three passages just in Genesis alone you will find God speaking and he's conversing with the fullness of His personhood:

*Genesis 1:27 "Let us make man,"*

*3:22 "Lord God said behold, the man has become as one of us,"*

*11:6, 7 "Let us go down"*

These passages cannot be viewed from the human perspective. When a man is talking to himself we understand that we are finite beings and even talking to ourselves we are limited in our total being involvement. God had a conversation with the fullness of His triune self. In harmonious agreement according to His will; yet they work at as one.

## The Characteristics of the Godhead

The Godhead never loses its essence of being one though separate in manifestations and duty; but they stay eternal. This shows that God is one in fulfilling His will and purpose. Let's examine some of the characteristics of each of the persons of the Godhead.

### God the Father

A. The Head of the God Head Co Equal with the Son and Holy Spirit.
B. God is a spirit John 4:24
C. Fundamental in redemption John 3:16
D. The gifter of the only Begotten John 3:16
E. First person at work at the origin of time Genesis 1:1
F. The designer of earth Genesis 1:1; Job 38-41

# The Son Christ Jesus

A. Second person of the Godhead equal to the Father and Holy Spirit.
B. The eternal word John 1:1
C. The Incarnation of God John 1:14, Isaiah 7:14
D. The only begotten John 3:16; Colossians 1:19
E. The perfect sacrifice Romans 3:25, I John 2:2
F. Resurrected Lord I Corinthians 15;19-22

# The Holy Spirit

A. Third person of the Godhead, equal to the Father and Son
B. Promised Comforter, teacher and Spiritual memory John 14:26
C. Convicts sin, Righteous and execute judgment John 16:7-11
D. He makes alive the Believer I John 2:20,27
E. He seals the believer II Corinthians 1:22; Ephesians 1:13
F. He bears witness of Jesus Christ I John 5:16

# Part II

## Salvation

For years I remember thinking that salvation meant agreeing about Jesus without understanding the significance, and the hope to go to heaven. I now understand why I left the church during my mid teens. For years I had no sense of hope or peace for eternal security. If I didn't study or be exposed to a teaching atmosphere, leaving the fellowship of any church became easy.

Why I felt this way? When struggles designed to test your faith occur, you are in for a fight. If you don't know who God is to you or understand your salvation; you will walk away from the faith. This happens because of the lack of understanding.

I'm not saying when you run into a trial in life you won't make it, but if you have not been equipped with understanding you can become disheartened.

Salvation illustrates God provision and the grace in which we are saved.

*"And the Lord God made clothing from animal skins for Adam and his wife".* Genesis 3:21

This is a comparison or typology of what Jesus was to perform for man in the future. God sacrificed an innocent animal by shedding its blood to cover Adam and Eve's shame. This is very important as we go through this book as we look further into salvation.

So what does salvation mean? In a recent online poll the responses I received were as follows.

Sharise L. "Eternity and life with Jesus by faith,"

Beverly W. "Eternal life,"

Evonne W. "Pray and forgiveness,"

LaTonya B. "Faith and eternal Life with Jesus,"

Are these answers wrong? Or are they just pieces of what Salvation means. God's process of salvation makes these answers incomplete.

## Salvation's Definition

Salvation means deliverance or redemption. What are we redeemed from?

Sins:

- Penalty
- Power
- Person
- Pleasure
- Presence
- Perpetuity (eternal separation)

We will break down the questions why God redeemed us from the ugliness of sin.

God is very thorough for reconciling man. He took every precaution. It's good to know God is all knowing. He covered all the bases to make sure we all have an opportunity to receive his greatest gift of love for us.

# Sin's Penalty

When God created Adam, He gave him specific instructions. He told him
*"But of the tree of the knowledge of good and evil thou shalt not eat of it; for in the day that thou eatest thereof thou shalt surely die "*Genesis 2:17.

Once Adam disobeys God the penalty comes at once. Adam experienced exactly what was declared, his death.

Adam's sin introduced to the world a three part death experience: Spiritual, Physical and Eternal. Death means separation, and the results were a penalty all men would now face because of a choice. Knowing God is a Holy God; his righteousness would not allow Him to have sin in His presence.

**Death:**

**Spiritual:** the spirit separated from God because of our sin nature and deeds in our body.

**Physical:** the separation of the soul from the body. God promised Adam that he return to the ground from where he was created.

*"In the sweat of thy face shalt thou eat bread, till thou return unto the ground; for out of it was thou taken: for dust thou art, and unto dust shalt thou return."* Genesis 3:19

**Eternal:** The separation of both body and soul cast into the lake of fire; eternally separated from God.

Revelations 20:15 *"And whosoever was not found written in the book of life was cast into the lake of fire,"*

Since we are born with a sin nature we have the same "death sentence" because of being descendants of Adam, we carry his flawed image.

"And Adam lived an hundred and thirty years and begat a son in his own likeness after his own image," Genesis 5:3a.

This image was sin that separates us and demands justice to be served. Understanding sin's penalty why would anyone reject God's gift of redemption?

# Sin's Power

Sin has an unusual effect on man.  Man's makeup is flesh, mind and spirit.  The challenge for man is surviving the battlefield of the mind and will.  At birth we are automatically under sins power; because of the original sin of Adam humanity is corrupt.

This affects the total man.  It affects our thoughts, emotions and actions.  The best way to describe the affects of sin is to compare it to a zombie, "The living dead".  This is truly an accurate description of humanity; spiritually we are the living dead.  This is our condition outside of the fellowship of God.

God took every measure to make sure sins power is defeated for those who embrace Christ.

*"We use God's mighty weapons, not merely worldly weapons, to knock down the devil's strongholds,"* II Corinthians 10:4 (NLT).

# Sins Person

Lucifer before the name and address change according to scripture he was:

*"The anointed cherub that covereth,"* Ezekiel 28:14a.

He is an angel of great beauty. He also had great influence because of his position. Knowing that angels are created beings, they are not to be worshipped.

Satan when in heaven wanted to exalt himself and was filled with pride.

*"For thou hast said in thine heart, I will ascend into heaven. I will exalt my throne above the stars of God: I will sit also upon the mount of the congregation in the side of the north; I will ascend above the heights of the clouds: I will be like the most High,"* Isaiah 14:13, 14.

God immediately addressed his rebellion and his fate.

*"Yet you shalt be brought down to hell, to the sides of the pit"* Isaiah 14:15. (Additional references Ezekiel 28:16; Luke 10:18)

Satan's plan since his fall has not changed. This plan destroys man.

*"Be careful! Watch out for attacks from the Devil, you enemy. He prowls around like a roaring lion looking for some victim to devour,"* I Peter 5:8 (NLT)

God is Holy and righteous and no sin is tolerated. God promised his defeat and prophesied how it would happen in the Garden of Eden.

*"I will put enmity between thee and the woman, and between thy seed and her seed; it shall bruise thy head, and thou shalt bruise his heel,"* Genesis 3:15.

With no doubt God is victorious over Satan and his enemies.

*"And the devil that deceived them was cast into the lake of fire and brimstone, where the beast and the False prophet are, and shall be tormented day and night forever and ever,"* Revelations 20:10.

If there was any doubt about God's provision for us, know in advance "God Wins" and punishes the person of sin as promised.

## Sins Pleasure

To resist sin takes discipline. It is not an easy task to resist the constant bombardment of sins influences. It is our make up to rebel; it's what our nature demands. The danger of this is that you can become engrossed in sin until you become calloused and God will get involved and allow your sinfulness to consume you.

*"When they refused to acknowledge God, He abandoned them to their evil minds and let them do things that should never be done. Their lives became full of every kind of wickedness, sin, greed, hate, envy, murder, fighting, deception, malicious behavior, and gossip. They are backstabbers, hater of God, insolent, proud, and boastful. They are forever inventing new ways of sinning and are disobedient to their parents. They refuse to understand, break their promises, and are heartless and unforgiving. They are fully aware of God's death penalty for those who do these things, yet they go right ahead and do them anyway. And, worse yet, they encourage others to do them, too."*

Romans 1:28-32 (NLT)

God's Promise for Salvation

God warns us not to love the pleasure of the
world. It is very dangerous to abide in sin and not
recognizing God's provision. To reject God and live
for the pleasure of the flesh means condemnation.

*"There is no judgment awaiting those who trust
him. But those who do not trust him have already
been judged for not believing in the only Son of
God. Their judgment is based on this fact: The light
from heaven came into the world, but they loved
the darkness more than the light for their actions
were evil."* John 3:18, 19 *(NLT)*

The judgments God has in place for sin are sure,
but God has made it clear to avoid sin. This part of
His provisions further shows just how much God
will do for man.

## Sins Presence

This is a glorious event, a glorious day.  God removing his believers from the atmosphere of sin; this is the hope for those who believe in the Lord Jesus Christ.

*"For the Lord himself will come down with a commanding shout with the call of the archangel, and with the trumpet call of God.  First, all the Christians who have died will rise from their graves. Then together with them, we who are still alive and remain on the earth will be caught up in the clouds to meet the Lord in the air and remain with him forever," I Thessalonians 4:16, 17. (NLT)*

This is called "the rapture" which means "caught up".

For those who are in Christ, we look forward to seeing our saviors face.  The only thing that makes this life worth living is the assurance of God's promise for his creation. I can't wait!

# Sins Perpetuity

## (Eternal damnation for the wicked)

This is for those who reject God's provision, eternal separation. Since Adam's disobedience in the Garden of Eden this had to be addressed. The Bible is clear those who don't believe and receive the gift of salvation will experience eternal separation from God.

Revelations 20:11-15 states...

*"And I saw a great white throne, and I saw the one who was sitting on it. The earth and sky fled from his presence, but they found no place to hide. I saw the dead, both great and small standing before God's throne. And the books were opened, including the Book of Life. And the dead were judged according to the things written in the books, according to what they had done. The sea gave up the dead in it, and death and the grave gave up the dead in them. They were all judged according to their deeds. And death and the grave were thrown into the lake of fire. Anyone whose name was not found recorded in the Book of Life was thrown into the lake of fire."* (NLT)

God's Promise for Salvation

There is nothing you can do at this point for rejecting Jesus Christ as Lord. There is no escaping this penalty.

# Part III

## Can Man Save Himself?

Since the fall of man, Adam and all generations are completely helpless for addressing sin. When Adam tried to address sin the first thing he did was make fig coverings for him and Eve.

*"At that moment their eyes were opened, and they suddenly felt shame at their nakedness. So they strung fig leaves together around their hips to cover themselves." Genesis 3:7 (NLT)*

Sin had created limitations in man; it affected his thoughts, emotions and will.

Adam thought he could change the result of his shame by making fig aprons or belts. Second Adam was in perfect fellowship with God and when he heard the voice of the Lord, Adam and Eve ran and hid among the trees.

*"Toward evening they heard the Lord God walking about in the garden so they hid themselves among the trees." Genesis 3:8 (NLT)*

Adam experienced fear and created distance between himself and God by hiding.

*"The Lord God called to Adam, Where are you?"* He replied, I heard you, so I hid. I was afraid because I was naked. Genesis 3:9, 10 *(NLT)*

Adam delivers the most absurd statement to God about His provision for him; he blames God about Eve after he has eaten the fruit that God warned him not to eat.

*"Yes. Adam admitted, but it was the woman you gave me who brought me the fruit and I ate it."* Genesis 3:12 *(NLT)*

Adams sin shows the inability to help himself or anyone else because of his reactions to what he had done. This is why God has to intervene on mans behalf.

God knowing the need of man sacrificed an innocent animal to cover Adam and Eve. This is a typology of Jesus sacrifice. It required the shedding of blood to make things right. It was the method that pleased the Father. As we look at Jesus it took the shedding of His blood to cover and pay our sin debt. It is the only sacrifice the Father.

*"For God made Christ, who never sinned, to be the offering for our sin, so that we could be made right with God through Christ."* II Corinthians 5:21 (NLT)

Man must make a choice to accept or reject the cover charge for sin's penalty. All men must understand the ugliness of sin; and by faith know that God's gift of salvation is available to me right now.

## How Was Salvation Provided?

God set all things in order. He has a perfect plan, and it works according to his will.

*"For God so loved the world, that he gave his only begotten son. That whosoever believes in him should not parish but have everlasting life."*
John 3:16 (NLT)

God loves his creation so much that the only thing he wants is to restore a broken relationship with man through Jesus.

God gave us a perfect gift to make things right, His son. He sent Him as the sacrifice for our sin. He was the perfect sacrifice without spot of blemish.

*"He paid for you with the precious lifeblood of Christ, the sinless, spotless Lamb of God."*
I Peter 1:19 (NLT)

Jesus came to take my place and pay for my sins on the cross.  Jesus took the shame, beatings, flogged and humiliation just for me.  Carried from courtroom to courtroom at night; lied on and sentenced to death for telling the truth.

Soldiers forced Him to carry his cross and marched Him to Golgotha's Hill (means place of the skull).  It is what God done for me. He shed his blood and died, was buried. As prophesied Jesus and rose from the dead.

*"I pass on to you what was most important and what had also been passed on to me, that Christ died for our sins, just as the scriptures* said.  *He was buried, and he was raised from the dead on the third day as the scriptures said. He was seen by Peter and then by the twelve apostles."*
I Corinthians 15:3-5 (NLT)

Then he ascended into heaven and seated on the right hand of the Father. His blood placed on the heavenly mercy seat.

*"When the Lord Jesus had finished talking with them, he was taken up into heaven and sat sown in the place of honor at God's right hand."*
Mark 16:19 (NLT)

*"Once for all time he took blood into the Most Holy Place, but not the blood of goats and calves. He took his own blood, and with it he secured our salvation forever."* (NLT)  Hebrews 9:12

The entire salvation process is all in God's hands. There is nothing man could do to obtain salvation based on his own efforts. God tells us that....

*"We are all infected and impure with sin. When we proudly display our righteous deeds, we find they are but filthy rags. Like autumn leaves, we wither and fall.  And our sins, like the wind, sweep us away."*  Isaiah 64:6 (NLT)

But Jesus is the sacrifice that pleases the Father.

*"Yet it pleased the Lord to bruise him; he hath put him to grief: when thou shalt make his soul an offering for sin, he shall see his seed, he shall prolong his days, and the pleasure of the Lord shall prosper in his hands,"*
Isaiah 53:10

# Part IV

## How Can I Receive The Gift Of Salvation?

How can I be saved? Do you want to be delivered or redeemed from sin and its effects? Here's how!

Repent: Total change of attitude about self, sin and God.

***What does this mean?***

Admitting that:

- I have sinned
  *"For all sinned a sinned and fall short of God's glorious standard,"* Romans 3:23 (NLT)
- I am a born sinner
  *"Because one person disobeyed God many people became sinners,"* Romans 5:19a (NLT)
- I am a helpless sinner
  *"And the person who keeps all of the law except one is as guilty as the person who has broken them all,"* James 2:10 (NLT)
- I deserve hell
  *"For the wages of sin is death, but the free gift of God is eternal life through Christ Jesus our Lord,"* Romans 6:23 (NLT)

- Only God can deliver me from Hell
  *"Victory comes from you O Lord. May your blessings rest on your people,"*
  Psalms 3:8 (NLT)
- Totally transfer all trust to Christ
  *"They replied, Believe in the Lord Jesus and you will be saved,"* Acts 16:31a (NLT)
  a. Believe who is
   *"No one has ever seen God. But his only Son, who is himself God, is near to the Father's heart; he has told us about him,"* John 1:18 (NLT)
  b. Believe what He's done for me personally
  *"But God showed his great love for us by sending Christ to die for us while we were sinners."* Romans 5:8 (NLT)
- By faith receive Jesus Christ into your heart as Savior and Lord.
  *"For if you confess with your mouth that Jesus is Lord and believe in your heart that God raised him from the dead, you will be saved. For it is by believing in your heart that you are made right with God. And it by confessing with your mouth that you are saved."* Romans 10:9,10 (NLT)

Here's a prayer if you desire to receive Jesus into your heart.

Dear Heavenly Father,

I come asking you for the forgiveness of sin. I believe I have sinned against you and that I am a sinner. I believe that I am a helpless sinner who deserves death and hell.

I recognize that only you can save me from my sin, and I totally transfer all trust and faith in your son Jesus Christ. I believe in my heart that Jesus was born, lived a sinless and died for my sin. That you raised Him from the dead bodily and was seen visibly by many witnesses.

I believe this in my heart and confess it with my mouth in the name of Jesus.

Amen.

**Follow the above steps you will be saved!**

**Part V**

## The Results of Salvation

There are instant changes that take place once you have confessed Jesus as Lord. Here's the list of those changes.

- You have forgiveness of sin.
  *"He is so rich in kindness that he purchased our freedom through the blood of his Son, and our sins are forgiven,"*
  Ephesians 1:7 (NLT)
- You have peace with God
  *"Therefore, since we have been made right in God's sight by faith, we have peace with God because of what Jesus Christ our Lord has done for us." Romans 5:1 (NLT)*
- *You have eternal security with Christ*
  *"I assure you, those who listen to my message and believe in God who sent have eternal life. They will never be condemned for their sins, but they have already passed from death into life." John 5:24 (NLT)*
- You have the Holy Spirit within you
  *"Or don't you know that your body is the temple of the Holy Spirit who lives in you and was given to you by God? You do not belong to yourself, for God bought you with*

God's Promise for Salvation

*a high price. So you must honor God with your body*," I Corinthians 6,19,20 (NLT)

- You have an intercessor in heaven
  *"My dear children, I am writing this to you so that you will not sin. But if you do sin, there is someone to plead for you before the Father. He is Jesus Christ, the one who pleases God completely."* I John 2:1 (NLT)

- You have an intercessor on earth
  *"And the Holy Spirit helps us in our distress. For we don't even know what we should pray for, nor how we should pray. But the Holy Spirit prays for us with groaning that cannot be express in words. And the Father who knows all hearts knows what the Spirit is saying for the Spirit pleads for us believers in harmony with God's own will."*
  Romans 8:26,27 (NLT)

- You are a child of God
  *"But to all who believed him and accepted him, he gave the right to become children of God."* John 1:12 (NLT)

**46** | P a g e

- You are a member of the body of Christ
  *"Some of us are Jews, some are Gentiles, some are slaves, and some are free. But we have all been baptized into Christ's body by one Spirit, and we have all received the same Spirit."* I Corinthians 12:13 (NLT)
- You are a new creation
  *"What this means is that those who become Christians become new persons. They are not the same anymore, for the old life is gone. A new life has begun."*
  II Corinthians 5:17 (NLT)
- You are a dual nature being (Old Man Vs. New Man in Christ Jesus)
  *"The old sinful nature love to do evil, which is just opposite from what the Holy Spirit wants. And the Spirit gives us desires that are opposite from what the sinful nature desires. These two forces are constantly fighting each other, and your choices are never free from this conflict. But when you are directed by the Holy Spirit, you are no longer subject to the law."*
  Galatians 5:17-19 (NLT)

- You are an ambassador for Christ
  *"We are Christ ambassadors, and God is using us to speak to you. We urge you as though Christ himself were here pleading with you, Be reconciled to God,"*
  II Corinthians 5:20
- You are joint heirs with Christ
  *"And since we are his children, we will share his treasures for everything God gives to his Son, Christ, is ours, too.  But if we are to share his glory, we must also share his suffering."*
  Romans 8:17 (NLT)

His grace towards us is free, and eternity is guaranteed.  From this point forward, it is our responsibility to continue to study God's word and continue growing.

# Part VI

## The Ordinances of the Church

Within the church there are two ordinances that believers in the body of Christ observe. They are Baptism and the Lords Supper. Both are very important, but neither one of these has any saving power. Both are symbolic of Events reflecting on the earthly work of Christ. Let's look at them closer.

## Baptism

Baptism means to dip or immerse. Baptism is symbolic of the death, burial and resurrection of Jesus. It is an outward declaration for believers that shows that we have died to their old sin nature, buried in a watery grave and resurrected in victory.

In the Bible we see our example of Jesus being baptized.

*"Then Jesus went from Galilee to the Jordan River to be baptized by John. But John tried to talk him out of it. I am the one who needs to be baptized by you," he said, "so why are you coming to me?" But Jesus said, "It should be done, for we must carry out all that God requires." So John agreed to baptize him.*

*After his baptism, as Jesus came up out of the water, the heavens were opened and he saw the Spirit of God descending like a dove and settling on him. And a voice from heaven said, "This is my dearly loved Son, who brings me great joy."* Matthew chapter 3:13-17 (NLT)

Jesus doing this was very important because of this we follow his example. Also this was the ministerial inauguration of Jesus. Jesus was getting ready to begin his three year ministry; and the countdown to being crucified for our sins.

After Jesus was raised from the dead, Jesus made an important commission to His Apostles.

*"Therefore go and make disciples of all the nations, baptizing them in the name of the Father and the Son and the Holy Spirit."* Matthew 28:19 (NLT)

I am careful to observe specific needs were someone may not be able to get baptized due to various reasons for example.

Jesus was crucified between two thieves and one began to mock him trying to avoid the penalty of his sin....death!

*"One of the criminals hanging beside Him scoffed So if you're the Messiah, are you? Prove it by saving yourself and us too while you're at it!" But the other criminal protested, "Don't you fear God even when you are dying? We deserve to die for our evil deed, but this man hasn't done anything wrong." Then He said "Jesus remember me when you come into your Kingdom." And Jesus replied, "I assure you today you will be with me in paradise."*

Luke 23:39-43 (NLT)

This man didn't have a chance to honor him through baptism. Yet he was saved just by his proclamation of faith in Jesus as Lord and savior. The man now a believer is proof that if you can't be baptized that it will not stop you from going to heaven. Jesus promised him at that moment he would be with Him in paradise.

Although there are rare occasions I encourage all who can to be obedient to the will of God and be baptized. Doing anything different than how Jesus commanded is being disobedient to His authority and what is required of us.

## The Last Supper/Communion

The other ordinance of Communion is commonly practiced within the faith. It was first instituted with the Nation of Israel celebrating the Passover feast when God delivered the Israelites from the bondage of the Egyptians.

They were instructed by Moses …

*"From now on, this month will be the first month of the year for you. Announce to the whole community that on the tenth day of this month each family must choose a lamb or a young goat for a sacrifice. This animal must be one year old male either a sheep or a goat with no physical defects. They are to take some of the lamb's blood and smear it on the top and sides of the doorframe of the house where the lamb will be eaten. That evening everyone must eat roast lamb with bitter herbs and bread without yeast."*
Exodus 12:2, 3,5,7,8 (NLT)

Looking at the New Testament reference; we find Jesus with his disciple's celebrating the Passover meal.

*"Jesus said, I have looked forward to this hour with deep longing, anxious to eat this Passover meal*

*with you before my suffering begins. For I tell you now that I won't eat it again until it comes to fulfillment in the Kingdom of God. Then He took a cup of wine and when he had given thanks for it he said Take this and share it among yourselves. For I will not drink wine again until the kingdom of God has come. Then he took a loaf of bread; and when he had thanked God for it, he broke it in pieces and gave it to the disciples, saying, "This is my body given for you. Do this in remembrance of me." After supper he took another cup of wine and said, "This wine is the token of God's new covenant to save you-an agreement sealed with the blood I will pour out for you." Luke 22:15-20*

I have to point out some things comparing the two passages. In the Exodus passage we find the conditions of the lamb or goat. Its age and without any defects; In Luke we see they have drink and bread but no lamb.

## Where Is The Lamb?

The lamb is not missing, it's not **on** the table, but he is **at** the table.  The lamb is Jesus, to be sacrificed without spot or blemish.  He is to shed his blood for our sins.  Notice again what he say's

*"This is my body given for you.  Do this in remembrance of me."*

*"This wine is the token of God's new covenant to save you-an agreement sealed with the blood I will pour out for you."*  Luke 22:19b, 20 (NLT)

Jesus is instituting this practice for us to remember his sacrifice, his death for our sins.  So when believers come together we are to remember the death of Jesus. The Apostle Paul mentions...

*"For every time you eat this bread and drink this cup, you are announcing the Lord's death until he comes again."* I Corinthians 11:26 (NLT)

The wine symbolizes the shed blood, and the bread symbolizes Jesus Body.  So when you are eating this you are partaking in the Lord's death. It is as Paul says announcing his death publically.

There are some warnings concerning observing the communion that the Apostle Paul mentions.

*"So if anyone eats this bread or drinks this cup of the Lord unworthily, that person is guilty of sinning against the body and the blood of the Lord. That is why you should examine yourself before eating the bread and drinking from the cup. For if you eat the bread or drink the cup unworthily, not honoring the body of Christ, you are eating and drinking God's judgment upon yourself. That is why many of you are weak and sick and some have even died. But if we examine ourselves we will not be examined by God and judged in this way,"*
I Corinthians 11:27-31 (NLT)

It is imperative that before you partake of the communion if you are not reflecting and honoring the body and blood of Jesus Christ I strongly suggest take time to repent your sin and then partake. God is very serious regarding his sacrifice and it should be revered.

As we continue to grow, it is imperative to study and gain a better understanding of God's word. While learning to understand the work of each person in the Godhead we develop a sense of closeness.

Most of all to know how God provided salvation for man, and that He is the only one who can deliver us. He provided what was needed to pay our sin debt through Jesus Christ and faith alone in Christ can save us.

Because we know how we are saved we should be better equipped to share how we are saved, and able to explain our faith, systematically and with boldness to our family, friends and strangers. Let us be encouraged to fulfill the commission our Savior.

*"Therefore go and make disciples of all the nations, baptizing them in the name of the Father and the Son and the Holy Spirit."* Matthew 28:19 (NLT)

Amen

# Notes

## Notes

# Thank You

I want to thank those who purchased and read this book. I pray that the information was informative and an encouragement to you. As you continue your faith walk I pray God continues to open up your understanding and your bond becomes stronger.

God Bless you all

Phillip Lane Sr.

# Contact the Author

If this book has truly made a difference in your life, I would love to hear from you. If you have any comments or questions or are requesting book signing information

Please contact me at: Website:

www.PhillipLaneMinistries.comFa

Email: Philliplanesr71@gmail.com

Facebook: Phillip Lane Sr.

Twitter: https://twitter.com/Philliplanesr71

Be on the lookout for more updates and books on the series of Christian Living.

41945645R00035

Made in the USA
Lexington, KY
11 June 2019